The Death
of
Teddy Ballgame

Also by Robert Mailer Anderson

Novels
Boonville

Film
Pighunt

MOLOTOV
EDITIONS

The Death of Teddy Ballgame

A Play

by Robert Mailer Anderson

WITH ILLUSTRATIONS BY SANDOW BIRK

MOLOTOV EDITIONS
SAN FRANCISCO, CA

MOLOTOV EDITIONS
5758 Geary Blvd. #221
San Francisco, CA 94121

www.molotoveditions.com

A version of *The Death of Teddy Ballgame* was previously published as a work-in-progress in *The Anderson Valley Advertiser* issues: October 14, 2009; October 21, 2009; October 28, 2009; November 4, 2009; November 11, 2009; and November 18, 2009.

Cover Design: Jay Walsh
Layout: Darcy Fray

Library of Congress Control Number: 2016911113
ISBN: 978-0-9967659-2-3

First Edition

10 9 8 7 6 5 4 3 2 1

For my wife Nicola, and my children
Dashiell, Lucinda, Frances, Callum, and Stephen.
Without them, there is no morning cup
of coffee.

And in loving memory of
Wilkes Bashford, Larry Sultan, Gay Barnes,
and
Jim Isaac.

ACT ONE

Cafe Dante. The near future. Morning.

*Three tired and disheveled men; **Karl** (50s) world-weary in an unwashed plaid shirt, **Dean** (30s) dumpy and earnest wearing a mismatched sweatsuit, **Marcus** (70s) Jewish and soft-spoken in a rumpled suit, sit at a table inside a coffee shop. Winter coats drape over the backs of their chairs.*

Their table is nearest the counter where there is a cash register, espresso machine, and condiments.

The other tables are empty.

An electric guitar and amplifier rest on a small stage by the last table. On the wall near the stage is a payphone.

"Cafe Dante" is painted in black letters on a window. The light outside the café has an ominous glow.

The men scrutinize the coffee cups in front of them...

Dean: You gonna drink that?

Karl: What do you think?

Dean: I don't know. How long can a guy go without drinking anything?

Marcus: *(pushes his cup away)* I am not going to drink anything that I know is a diuretic.

Dean: Diuretic?

Marcus: Anything that promotes the production of urine by the kidney.

Dean: *(scowls)* Coffee does that?

Marcus nods.

So, no coffee, no pastry. And we got no newspaper. *(sighs)* This is some morning.

Karl: *(scoffs)* Newspaper?

Dean: We need to know what's going on, don't we?

Karl: What decade are you living in?

Dean shrugs.

Newspapers. The golden age of *misinformation*. Propaganda. Horoscopes and gossip delivered to your doorstep.

Marcus: It beats Fox News and Wikipedia. Heresay and collective delusion disguised as facts.

Karl: A newspaper is just a perspective. Reporters get paid. So do editors.

Marcus: Three sources. Fact checkers. Not just opinion. That's op-ed.

Karl: A newspaper has to sell ads. *The New York Times*, the newspaper of record, "all the news that's fit to print," is, I mean *was*, fifty-one percent advertising.

Marcus: Journalism is the lynch pin of democracy. And if you'd read the foreign press, you'd have got a different story.

Karl: I'll tell you today's headlines worldwide: Blah Blah Blah. Some photos. Rubble and fire. The dead piled high. Disaster codified, in color with a pie chart.

Dean: There'd be more to it. What our leaders were saying...

Karl: The ones two miles underground? *(stands up, makes his hands into a pretend megaphone)* "We will not be defeated. Our spirit is indomitable." *(sits down)* Recycled pep talks. What did the mayor of Nagasaki say? *Seattle? Baghdad?* I'd rather hear Nero fiddle.

Dean: At least they'd tell us what to do.

Marcus: I've been told enough. When I can travel, where… With their *lists.* Detention centers. Hooded accusers.

Karl: We *did* what they told us to do. Look outside. *Mission accomplished.*

The men look outside at the glow.

Marcus: If you don't know what's *been done,* you can't know what to do.

Karl: The *koan* of the day.

Dean: I still think we need a newspaper.

Marcus: We need *journalism.*

Karl: Too late. Most people couldn't fill in a blank map of the world let alone name a country's dominant religion, a nation's imports and exports. Trade routes. We should have been reading economics, science books...

Marcus: *History.*

Karl: Paying less attention to sports and the sex lives of celebrities.

Dean pours sugar into his coffee, as a shadow of a person sprints by the café window.

Now the map *is* blank. Matching our knowledge of the world.

Dean: I happen to like sports.

Karl: So do I. But pop quiz, where's Mauratania? What's the capital? What's their religion?

Dean looks blank.

Go ahead, drink your coffee.

All three men stare at their coffee as the shadows of two military men holding guns race by the window. One shouts, but the men are unfazed by the commotion.

Marcus: Mauritania is in Africa. Northwest Africa. A Muslim people that took their independence from France. I don't know the capital, desert sand and a sirocco wind. It's a wasteland. But what isn't now?

Dean fiddles with his cup.

Dean: If our cellphones worked we could log onto the blogosphere.

Marcus: Diaries masquerading as truth.

Dean: What about the weather? The daily forecast?

Karl: I'd say its thirty degrees colder than it should be this time of year. With a chance of raining frogs.

An emergency siren blares.

A recorded message plays on a PA system outside: "Crisis code BLACK. Terror alert RED. Only authorized personnel may cross into colored sectors. Stay in your home zone. Report any terrorist activity to police immediately, including suspicious behavior. We will not be defeated. Our spirit is indomitable..."

Every hour on the hour.

Marcus leans towards his coffee cup and inhales deeply, savoring the scent.

Marcus: I remember the Cuban Missile Crisis. You both are too young. Kennedy and Khrushchev. A chess match. Fisher versus Spassky. We practiced for a nuclear attack by crawling underneath school desks.

Marcus takes the saucer from beneath his cup and places it on top like a lid.

Every family had an emergency supply of canned goods and water. We listened on our transistor radios for the Russian ships to turn around. Pawn to king four.

Holding it by the handle, Marcus turns his coffee cup in a circle.

I've been prepared for this inevitability. Somewhat.

Dean: Do you still got that stuff? Maybe your water is good. And we could make an *un*diuretic.

Marcus: I live upstairs now, in the hotel. I don't have any supplies.

Dean: You're upstairs too, right Karl? You got any emergency supplies?

Karl: I've got a sink I pee in when I'm too lazy to walk down the hall.

Dean: I've used that sink...

Karl looks at Dean, raising an eyebrow.

That's gross. A grown man should walk to the bathroom.

Karl takes out a pack of cigarettes and a Zippo lighter.

Karl: That's how Lenny Bruce's defense attorney selected his jury. He asked them if they had ever peed in a sink. What do you think they said?

Dean: Who's Lenny Bruce?

Karl: *(lights cigarette)* He's a diuretic.

Karl takes a drag from the cigarette.

Dean: You're not supposed to smoke in here.

Karl: You'd be lucky to live long enough to die from some cancer caused by my second-hand smoke. Or some lurgy from my piss.

Karl extends the pack to Marcus who takes a cigarette. Karl lights it for him. They both take drags.

What I remember is Vietnam, on TV.

Marcus: When they could show war in the news. Soldier's dead bodies...

Karl: Villages being napalmed. My father would curse and my mom would try not to cry. We watched, hoping for an image of my older brother, heroic and unscathed. *(beat)* Then we got a knock on the door, and they thanked us for his *service. (beat)* But all that happened over there. Some far off jungle place.

Dean: You had a brother?

Karl: Two. The other was in LA when... you know. Forget about it.

Karl stamps out the cigarette on the saucer.

Dean: When did they stop showing wars on the news?

Marcus: When our *leaders* demanded consensus without thought.

Dean: I saw the World Trade Center go down on TV.

Marcus: Exactly. The Big Lie.

Karl: Cheney's handiwork.

Dean: Cheney who?

Marcus: It seems like child's play now, doesn't it? Two brothers.

Karl: What?

Marcus: Excuse me, Karl, I meant to say, two buildings. The jets. *Box cutters.*

A figure approaches from outside – its shadow becoming larger and ghoulish in the café window.

Now all New York is a necropolis.

With a jingle of bells, **Terry** *(20s) attractive and wiry, enters the café. He appears tired, but full of nervous energy – rubbing his hands together from the cold.*

Terry: It's fuckin' spooky out there. *(looks at the men)* It's fuckin' spooky in here.

The men nod, "Hello."

I knew this place would be open. If there's one thing you can count on, it's coffee in your cup.

Terry sees there's no counter person.

Who's jocking coffee? Where's Paul, that little spiv?

Dean: Paul? He said he'd be right back.

Terry: "With electricity comes responsibility!"

Terry walks to the register, forming a line of one. He slaps his hands rhythmically on the counter. He sniffs at the air.

Terry: Who's been smoking?

Dean: These two. Not me.

Terry: Good for them. *New World Order.* The environmentalist can blow me too. *Recycling? Composting?* I sorted through my trash for years. For what? Fuck it. These are The Last Days. I'm throwing my garbage straight into my neighbor's back yard, that bull dyke Green Party bitch. If it start's fall-out snowing, like they say it's gonna, I'm wearing fur head to toe. Baby seal muckalucks.

Terry notices the men aren't drinking their coffee.

Why aren't you drinking your coffee?

Karl: Why do you think?

Terry's body slumps dramatically.

Terry: Fuck, fuck, fuck! *(stretches his arms as if being crucified)* I need my morning cup of coffee. I need two fuckin' cups of my morning cup of coffee. *(brings a hand to his head)* My head is throbbing.

Marcus: You can have mine. I just need the smell.

Terry: What?

Terry drops his arms to his side.

9

Marcus: You can have mine. I just need the smell.

Terry: I'm not drinking that shit if nobody else is. What do I look like, a *Croat*?

Dean: I might drink mine. When Paul gets back.

Marcus: I don't need to drink the coffee. It's just part of my routine; I shower, I shave, I walk to the café, I order... I sit. The *smell* wakes me up. My day has started.

Dean: A creature of habit.

Terry: An imbecile. I need to *drink* my fuckin' coffee.

Terry removes his jacket and drapes it on a chair at the men's table. He moves around the café, looking pained.

Karl: Hung over?

Terry: No. I didn't drink anything last night, except a few glasses of wine to compliment any other horrible events that might occur.

Dean: *(to Marcus)* What happens if the café closes?

Marcus: The café is not closing.

Dean: Paul might not come back.

Karl: *(to Terry)* What other horrible events?

Terry picks up the guitar at the stage, sits down on a chair and begins playing softly. No tune is discernible.

Terry: No *other* horrible events, just more of the same. But faster. SARS III, small pox, hurricanes...

Dean: The café could be closed and we don't even know it.

Terry: The air. The water. Seattle. Shang Hai. *Vegas*. Cats spreading plague. Who would have thought of that? Today it's no coffee.

Dean: And Paul could close the café if nobody drinks the coffee.

Marcus: He has a responsibility. People will come to the café.

Dean: Not if there's no coffee.

Terry: Tomorrow, there's nothing left horrible to happen but the end of the world. And without *coffee* that might not be so bad.

Marcus: Even without coffee, people will come.

Terry: *(to Karl)* So, Marcus is the optimist now? Lucky I got this girl, Theresa, with a fallout shelter full of wine. Twenty centimeters of concrete and lead. Otherwise, I wouldn't have drank that dago red. Fuckin' seeds and stems.

Marcus: In the middle ages, with all the open sewers, everyone drank beer and wine.

Terry: Her father was in that retro Cineplex downtown, one of the early biological attacks.

"The café could be closed and we don't even know it."

Karl: Tough break.

Terry: I'll say. A Julia Roberts movie. Erin Brockovich. *(laughs)* So that's what you get. Me screwing your daughter, drinking your wine.

Karl: I suppose you've never been to the movies?

Terry: Not since all this shit started.

Karl: What? The beginning of time?

Terry: I appreciate the long view, Karl, but no, not *the beginning of time*. You know what I'm talking about. No theaters for me. No tall buildings or airports. No hospitals, *places of worship*, mass transit, tunnels, bridges. I can't tell you the last time I opened my mail, before it stopped coming. Nothing but bills anyway. And anthrax. I don't know which is worse.

Dean: People got to go somewhere.

Marcus: Nothing is more natural.

Terry begins noodling again on the guitar, head down.

Terry: Like I'm gonna pay bills. The companies don't even exist. Scam artists waiting to cash checks. And what's money now? Something for the cockroaches. They can blow me too, if they think I'm leaving behind a balanced checkbook. They'll be lucky to get half a pack of Top Ramen.

Karl: So, what do you do then? Sit at home and jerk off?

Terry: Well, there's no Sports Center. And at least I know where I've been. I wear surgical gloves too. For *extra protection.*

Karl: I don't need the burden of that knowledge. Or the visual.

Terry: I'm telling you, if my dick falls off, that's the real end of the world. I traded a broken flashlight for a box of surgical gloves from one of those black market wandering entrepreneurs. Better safe than sorry.

Karl: There's an expression you used to hear more often.

Terry turns up the amp and cuts loose with the refrain to Queen's "We Are The Champions."

He suddenly stops.

Terry: Last night I broke down with Theresa, despite all the health warnings. I'll take Chlamydia over swine flu any day.

Terry plays an angry discordant riff.

Dean: You're in a bad mood.

Terry: *Well... (points outside)* That'll bring you down with a thump. And I have a fuckin' headache the size of a Russian tank.

Marcus: Quit playing that guitar.

Terry: And there's no coffee.

Karl: Marcus offered you his.

Terry: I ain't drinking that shit.

Dean: So, you got a hangover, huh?

Terry: No, Dean. I have a *headache*.

Karl: He was drinking with Theresa.

Dean: Who's Theresa?

Karl: His twin sister.

Terry: Fuck you, Karl. And half a bottle of wine isn't drinking.

Dean: Drinking wine is too drinking. And who's Theresa?

Terry: Drinking wine is not too drinking. People in France, *former* Europeans, drank wine with every meal and that was not considered drinking.

Marcus: The *French*.

Terry: They had better hearts because of it.

Karl: But you have a hangover.

Terry: Headache.

Terry sets down the guitar.

Dean: Drinking wine in France is still drinking wine even in France. Now, c'mon, who's Theresa?

15

Terry: Peter Piper picked a peck of pickled peppers, Dean. It's lucky for us that one rocket scientist survived Operation Freedom. If we need the obvious stated, the *reflexive property of equality* recited, we've got you sitting right here. There's still hope.

Dean: There is hope. And drinking wine is too drinking. And I don't care who Theresa is anymore.

Terry walks to the front door and looks outside.

And even without coffee, people will come to this café.

Terry: I don't see anybody coming, Nostradamus. I wouldn't have come if I knew there wasn't any coffee.

Terry shuts the door.

Dean: Bull fuck. You come here everyday to bitch and brag. That's how you wake up.

Terry: *(turns menacingly to Dean)* What did you say?

Dean: I said every morning you come in that door and tell us how much you drank and who you slept with...

Terry: Fuck you.

Karl: *(laughs)* He's right, Terry.

Terry: Fuck you. I came here for coffee.

Dean: Then drink it.

Terry: I said, "Fuck you!"

Terry walks over and peers into Marcus' coffee cup.

That's a buncha bullshit. *(to Karl)* Give me a fuckin' cigarette, will you?

Karl hands Terry a cigarette and the lighter.

At least I have some fun, you know? At least I'm not dead yet.

Marcus: I'm fine as long as there's coffee in my cup. I just need the smell.

Marcus picks up the saucer covering his cup and sniffs. Then he places the saucer back on the cup.

My day has started.

Terry: *(shakes lighter angrily)* Who cares about your fuckin' day?

Karl: There's no reason to get upset at Marcus.

Terry tries to get the lighter to work using "bar tricks," snapping his fingers across the wheel, rubbing the lighter against his leg, etc. Each one fails.

Terry: I'm not upset. I just don't have any coffee and my head is fuckin' pounding. And...

Terry gestures to the outside.

Karl: I think we're all upset because we *have* our coffee, we just can't drink it.

Dean: What's the difference?

17

Marcus: Because we are presented with a *choice*. That's what's maddening. Man longs deepest for those things he doesn't have. The unknown. The thirst for knowledge has always been our undoing.

Terry: Explain Starbucks then, my philosophical friends. Or McDonald's. *Billions* served. Why? People didn't go there searching for the *unknown*.

Marcus: No, they went out of fear. Fear of making the wrong choice.

Dean: That's why those companies were so successful?

Karl: That and they basically sold drugs.

Terry: What about TV? Six hundred channels of the same shit on twenty-four hours a day.

Marcus: Same principle. People fearing the moral consequences of making a decision. Any decision. Because making a decision means making a *choice*, and a choice means we *are responsible for who we are*. Most people don't want that responsibility, or the suffering that comes with it. But it is inalienable to man.

Terry: Oh, please Spinoza, enough. People went to McDonald's because it was cheap and they wanted a cheeseburger. If there was a Starbucks around here...

Dean: I'm not afraid of *choice*. I just know what I like. And I like what I *know*.

Terry: I know I like coffee. And if it didn't exist, I would goddamn brave the unknown and make a *choice* to invent it. Like somebody else already did.

Karl: I thought that was God man would invent if *He* didn't exist.

Terry: Same fuckin' thing. Because if the alarm goes off in the morning and there's no coffee, let me tell you, there's no God. God is dead.

Karl: What about contaminated coffee? A contaminated God?

Terry: No, not a contaminated God, Karl. A sick God. A sick fuckin' Wagnerian type God, wandering around with his own set of problems and deficiencies. One species above man. *(indicates the ranking with a hand motion)* Plants, animals, man, Gods. Your God. *(gestures the highest mark)* My God.

Dean: Do you think there will be a heaven if we blow up the earth?

Terry: No, Dean. And you won't get to meet your dead pets when you die either.

The payphone rings, surprising the men. Karl quickly moves to answer it.

Karl: *(into phone)* Hello. Hello?

Terry: Is that the big man Himself?

Karl: Can you hear me?

Terry: A payphone, how quaint.

Karl: Nobody's there.

Terry: You expecting a call?

Karl: *(lost in thought)* What?

Terry: Phones aren't exactly ringing off their hooks these days.

Karl puts the receiver back in the cradle. He walks slowly back to his seat.

What would you rather have, a H.A.M. Radio or a ham sandwich?

The shadows of two military men reappear, dragging a man.

Dean: I wish Paul would get here.

Terry tosses the lighter and unlit cigarette onto the table.

Terry: Fuck it. This is nonsense. I've been coming in here everyday for what? Eight years?

Marcus: Five years. You began patronizing this establishment five years ago.

Terry: Bullshit. Seven, at least.

Dean: Marcus said five.

Terry: What is he, Father Time? Over half a decade, I've been coming in here. Longer than Dean went to the junior college.

Dean: *Community college.* I went to the community college for five years.

Terry: Easy, Junior. This isn't semantics class.

Karl: Marcus is usually right.

Terry: I don't care if Marcus is usually right. My point... my point. I forgot my fuckin' point. Maybe that wine I drank last night *was* toxic.

The men snigger.

I bet I have a brain tumor.

Dean: The first symptoms are headaches.

Terry scowls at Dean, then puts his cigarette back in his mouth and again tries the lighter.

Terry: Fuck you guys. You know what? I'm drinking the coffee. How about that, my *good friends?* It's not even a question of faith, I need something with an "eine" in it to start *my* day; caffeine, nicotine, Benzedrine.

Terry finally gets the lighter to flame.

Dean: You're not supposed to smoke in here.

Terry: What are you, The Last American Hall Monitor?

Looking directly at Dean, Terry lights his cigarette. He takes a puff, and then glances down at Marcus's coffee.

Karl: Go ahead, Socrates. Drink up.

Terry takes another pull of his cigarette, then replaces Marcus's saucer beneath the cup – looking at the coffee as if he is about to lift something heavy.

Dean: I thought you said you were gonna drink it.

Marcus: I don't need to drink the coffee. The smell wakes me up.

Terry: We heard that Marcus. We are all very proud of your *transcendence*, your llama-like qualities. We are aware that Marcus doesn't need to drink the coffee. But we are all going to have to drink something, barring divine intervention. Sooner or later.

Terry lifts the cup, sniffing at the coffee.

Dean: So, you don't think the coffee's good either, huh?

Terry: I don't *know* if the coffee's good.

Karl: You're not drinking it.

Terry: I will. *Sometime.* Maybe not right now *(puts the cup down)*, because I've got this cigarette. But *sometime* I will drink the coffee. Even shaman Marcus will drink the coffee because we are *all* human.

Marcus: I get up, I shower, I shave...

Dean: How do you know shaving's safe?

Marcus: What?

Dean: If the water's contaminated, shaving might not be safe.

Karl: Showering would be worse.

Terry: Where's the start of your day now, Marcus?

Marcus: I can do without a shower.

Dean: How?

Terry: He can stand in the stall with no water and his *loofah*, and pretend.

Karl: How long can any of us go without bathing?

Terry: Dean, this is your field.

Dean: I don't need to drink coffee, but I need to take a shower.

Terry: You certainly do. You needed to shower long before the pubic service announcements. But who takes showers anymore? I should have showered because of my *interlude (makes a sexual gesture with his hips)*, not that I'm bragging, but I didn't.

Karl: Very European. Consistent with your wine intake. You might be able to get citizenship in one of the Benelux countries.

Marcus: They once trafficked in the gold teeth of my ancestors.

Terry: *(flicks an ash)* I won't miss any country that ate Nutella.

Karl: I know it's not right, but I always think of wooden shoes and tulips.

Terry: That's not a civilization.

Marcus: In my book, they are as good as the French.

Dean: Where's Benelux?

Terry: South of I-don't-give-a-damn.

Dean: What about Mauritania? Do you know where Mauritania is, Terry?

Terry: Don't fuck with me, Dean.

Dean shifts his gaze out the window.

I'm not showering, I'm not drinking the fuckin' coffee...

Marcus: My day has already started.

Terry tosses his cigarette into Dean's coffee cup.

Terry: Mine too.

Dean doesn't see Terry's cigarette. He continues looking out the window as outside another eerie shadow approaches. **Paul** *(30s), Asian and effeminate, enters holding a suitcase and a brown bag.*

Dean: You came back!

Paul: "With electricity comes responsibility."

Paul walks behind the counter, sets down his suitcase and the brown bag. He takes off his coat.

But I'm leaving after my shift. This sector closes in about three hours. And I need some coffee beans for the road. *(slips on apron)* Why are you smoking in here?

Terry: Pleasure and nicotine.

Dean: I told them, "No Smoking." But they didn't listen to me.

Terry: Yes we did. We just made the *choice* to keep smoking.

Dean: Hey Paul, when you leave is the café closed?

Marcus: It's not for him to decide.

Paul: Right now, the café is open. And while I'm working, the rules still apply: No smoking.

Marcus stamps out his cigarette.

Terry: Rules? Café? There's not even any fuckin' coffee.

Paul: I'll make you one. Double espresso?

Karl: He means we can't drink the coffee.

Paul: Why can't you drink the coffee?

The men gesture to the glow outside.

Karl: We realized it probably wasn't any good, right after you left.

Paul: Because of what happened to the reservoirs?

Karl shrugs.

But we have to eat and drink something.

Terry: I'd do it in a blue zone. Loot an Olive Garden.

Dean: Terry drank some wine last night from a bomb shelter.

Terry: When Theresa gets here, I'm going back to see if she's got any Folger's Crystals.

Paul: The coffee should be good. I filled the espresso machine with bottled water from the fridge.

Karl: BPA-free plastic?

Paul: There's heat from the espresso machine.

Marcus: Radiation is not bacteria. Heat won't kill it.

Paul removes a Geiger counter from the brown bag.

Dean: Where'd you get that?

Terry: The techies Ubered it over in a driverless car.

Paul: Infomercial. Like everybody else after *Vegas*. Before Amazon's drones got hacked.

Paul walks to their table and passes the Geiger counter over a cup of coffee. It makes a crackling sound. He waves it over the next cup.

These are okay.

Paul waves it over Dean's coffee - it crackles.

I wouldn't drink yours.

Terry: Ha!

Dean: Why?

Paul: There's a cigarette butt in it.

Dean looks at the butt in his coffee, then at Terry.

Dean: Otherwise it's fine?

Paul nods.

So, the café isn't closed?

Marcus: What did I tell you?

Terry: I'm telling you, let's celebrate. Make mine a double, Paul. Packed tight and pulled short. *Restretto.*

Dean: Could you make me another Americano?

Paul picks up Dean's cup and saucer.

Paul: You want a fresh one, Marcus?

Marcus: No thank you. I just needed the smell.

Dean: But now you can *drink* the coffee.

Marcus: My day has already started.

Terry shakes his head.

Paul: *(to Karl)* How about you?

Karl: I'm all right. But can I see that?

He gestures to the Geiger counter.

Paul: Careful with it.

Paul hands it to Karl, then returns to his post.

Karl looks at the instrument, then waves the Geiger counter over his coffee. Satisfied with the results, he sets down the Geiger counter and raises his cup.

Karl: To life's little pleasures. *(sips coffee)* Ahhhhh.

Terry rubs his hands together, anticipating his own drink.

Paul: Have any of you heard from your families?

Dean: My mother was in a green sector in Colorado but there was fallout from New Mexico. We were e-mailing before the band virus epidemic and made one of those rendezvous lists with *reunion dates*. But I don't know after this week. And last night.

Paul hands Dean's coffee to Terry who prankishly sticks his fingers into the cup without anybody noticing.

He wipes his fingers dry on his pants, and then passes the coffee to Dean.

Karl waves the Geiger counter over it, then nods that the coffee is okay.

Dean sips his coffee as Terry smiles, mischievously.

Paul: How about you, Terry?

Terry: *(becomes serious)* Gone. All fuckin' gone. A sister maybe. Part of the Feb 1st airlift. Talk about out of the frying pan into the fire. Aside from Vegas, right? Why not just book a flight straight to hell?

Paul hands Terry his coffee.

Paul: My family's heading to Canada. A road opened through the blue zones after the AI sweep. First one in twenty days.

Dean: Everybody says Southern Alberta.

Terry: A buncha cancer victims huddled in sub-zero climate.

Karl: At least there's no mosquitos.

Karl passes the Geiger counter over his body, looking at the meter. Then waves it over Dean, who cringes.

Marcus: Survival is an instinct.

Terry: So is beating a dead horse. Or caribou. Or moose. Or whatever the fuck they got up there. How about dying with dignity?

Terry shoots back his espresso.

Fuck!

He doubles over at his waist, hands on his stomach.

MOTHER FUCKER!

The men look worried.

Terry suddenly straightens up – smiling.

I fuckin' love coffee! Now *my* day has started.

Relieved, Karl and Dean sip their coffee.

Dean: What about you, Karl?

Karl: My daughter? My ex-wife? *(glances at payphone)* I don't want to talk about it.

Marcus: It's interesting what becomes our commonplace sorrow. What we can and cannot bear.

Marcus gestures to Karl, asking to use the Geiger counter. Karl hands it to him. Marcus inspects it, then passes the wand over objects around the table as he speaks.

It used to be an accident, a skidding car. Soiled innocence, perhaps. But how can we wake up one morning and have no family? To gather around a table with our morning coffee and say, today *all* of our wives are dead. Today, *all* of our children are dead. Today, *all* of our *grand*children are dead. Today, I have nobody.

He passes the Geiger counter over himself – frowning.

Today, *I* will die.

He sets the Geiger counter down.

Terry: I'm not dying today. And that ain't just the coffee talking.

Dean: There's hope.

Paul: Air currents in Alberta...

Terry: Fuck that. Theresa and a fallout shelter full of wine are *two blocks away.* And there's nothing like global tragedy to get a girl in the mood.

Marcus: *(more to himself)* I lost my wife to a cancer.

Terry: Theresa and I ain't married.

Marcus: My Elaine was sixty-five. That, at least, is a life. My children were forty, and thirty-eight. Their children, my seven grandchildren... You cannot *process* this, as they say.

Paul: Right now, I'd settle for living until I was sixty-five.

Karl: I would too, if I knew my daughter were alive. If I could find her.

Terry: I'm not settling for shit. But when the wine runs out and it turns into "Night of the Living Dead" outside, fuck it, I'll kill myself.

Paul: I couldn't kill myself.

Dean: It's a sin.

Paul: It'd hurt.

Karl: I'd settle for seeing Shelly to her twenty-fifth birthday. A father should be able to do that.

Terry: Or if those small pox fuckers show up like some long lost Mandan tribe trying to give back their blankets...

Dean: Zombies.

Paul: Lepers with no island.

Terry: Fuck that, they got *Long Island*. I heard some migrated as far west as Minnesota.

Marcus: It's horrific.

Terry: I know, Minnesota sucked already.

Dean: I'd still like to live forever.

Terry: In heaven? Or on earth? Because I *never* wanted to live forever. Not even *before*. Getting up every morning for eternity? Coffee isn't that good. *Sex* isn't that good. There's not enough to do, even with cable and an Xbox. Especially when you're some old geezer in a wheelchair *beshatting* yourself.

Marcus: Maybe that's why all this is happening. A last variation.

Dean: Did you get to have any funerals, Marcus? For your family?

Marcus: Some of my grandchildren were not buried. Children decomposing in a playground because there are too many others. Some only shadows, after the flash of an explosion.

Karl: *(more to himself)* My Shelly was twenty miles south of Chicago. She has a chance.

Another grotesque shadow approaches outside in the window.

Marcus: How do you bury a shadow?

With the ringing of bells, **Crimins** *(40), a survivalist with a redneck accent, enters the café.*

Unlike the others, Crimins is clean shaven and well-rested. He sports a crew cut, camouflage clothing, a gun belt with gun, ammo, also a knife, canteen, a Geiger counter, etc...

His pants are tucked into shiny black military boots. He wears reflective sunglasses.

Terry: *(indicates Crimins)* Another reason not to live forever. The planet's gonna be crawling with *Criminses.*

Karl: How is it that innocent children die, and he gets to live?

Crimins takes his sunglasses off, and surveys the café as if he has just topped a mountain peak.

Crimins: Preparation. Vigilance. Cunning.

He puts his sunglasses into one of his pockets, then sits at an empty table.

Paul: Hey, don't get too comfortable. You're not allowed in here.

Crimins: What ever happened to good morning?

Terry: This isn't a good morning.

Crimins: I'm talkin' etiquette. *(stares at Paul)* This great country took a turn for the worse when politeness took a backseat to liberal politics. "Give us your tired, give us your poor..." and they won't learn our language, say good morning, or look you in the eye.

Paul: I'm looking you in the eye, and I'm telling you, I didn't serve you *before* the apocalypse and I'm not serving you now.

Dean: Come on, Paul, "With electricity, comes responsibility."

Paul: *(points to the door)* Out, Crimins!

Crimins: You all don't want to face the facts. There's the coffee, but you don't want to wake up and smell it.

Dean: Marcus smelled his.

Crimins: Remember, I was the one that told you *all this* was going to happen?

The men roll their eyes and shake their heads – annoyed.

This country stood for so many things to so many different people that in the end we stood for nothing. We fell to our knees before peoples who have always hated us. They thrived on our milk and honey, and then seized on our lack of conviction.

"There's the coffee, but you don't want to wake up and smell it."

Terry: Peoples?

Crimins: How many immigrants grabbed a piece of the pie, then took another one home in a doggie bag? Liberals worried about every damn nation but our own. The Japs, Krauts, Arabs, Muslims, Israelis, they don't have any bleeding heart welfare for freeloaders that ain't of their creed.

Karl: So, everything that's happened is a result of U.S. immigration policy?

Crimins: Everything is a result of tribalism and natural selection. We let our sons and daughters be slaughtered to save someone else's aunts and uncles. How smart is that?

Paul: We fought our wars so we could continue to consume seventy percent of the world's resources...

Crimins: Liberal horseshit! Comin' from a Chinaman too. The worst environmental offenders.

Terry: Put a sock in it, Crimins.

Crimins: You think I'm the enemy? And Mr. Hebe and Mr. Gook there are your brothers? Because they drink coffee with you? Well, the coffee has been poisoned, sir.

Dean: No, the coffee's all right.

Paul: Did he just call me a *gook*?

Crimins: They used to want a melting pot. Then a *tossed salad*. Then that wasn't good enough. They wanted us to pray to Mecca and eat kosher with chopsticks.

Terry: You listened to a lot of talk radio, didn't you?

Crimins: You walk down the street lately? Over the bodies and broken glass?

Dean: I had to run from a gang to get here.

Crimins: We gave them the tools, the education, the *gold leaf party invitation* to destroy us. And that's just what they did. Because when it was Us versus Them, we said, "Why can't we all get along?" But that ain't the name of the game, Sonny Jim. This ain't no Sunday go to meeting. It's war!

Paul: Enough! Out, Crimins!

Crimins: We had a job to do, and we didn't do it.

Paul: Get out of this café!

Paul moves around the counter towards Crimins – holding a steel espresso group in his hand like a weapon.

Crimins: We got soft.

Paul: I want you out!

Crimins pulls a semi-automatic handgun from its holster.

Crimins: There was killing that needed to be done, and we couldn't stomach to pull the trigger.

He cocks the gun - pointing it at Paul who freezes.

I ain't afraid to pull a trigger.

Terry quickly scrambles away from Crimins.

Terry: Whoa, Crazy Man!

Dean: Holy shit!

Crimins stands calmly, pointing the gun at Paul.

Crimins: I've pulled triggers.

Paul raises his hands in submission.

Marcus: Put that gun away, young man.

Crimins: If it were up to me, there would be a *different* story to tell. You could walk down the street. You could love thy *neighbor*. People would say, "Good morning" when you met them for your cuppa.

Karl: *(stands up)* Calm down, Crimins.

Crimins points the gun at Karl.

Crimins: I am calm.

Karl: Paul hasn't done anything to you.

Crimins: What's that in his hand? A day-old cruller?

Paul looks at the espresso group, as if he doesn't know how it got into his hand.

Paul: I didn't mean anything by it.

Crimins: You told me, *directly*, "Get out." Ready to assault me with that hunk of steel. That's just what I'm saying, here's this homosexual chinaman in charge of my coffee shop, telling me, I've got to go.

Dean: He does have a responsibility, Karl. Because of the generator...

Karl: Shut up, Dean!

Crimins: I bet you celebrate Chinese New Year.

Paul: I celebrate both, regular *and* Chinese New Year.

Crimins: That's too much dressing on *my* tossed salad.

Paul: What kid doesn't like fireworks?

Crimins: You like fireworks? Now you're gonna see some.

Terry: Why don't you take this outside? There's a nice alley down the street, perfect for this kind of shit.

Crimins: *(to Terry)* No stomach for the killing. Liberal bitch dog politics. Lay on your back, paws up.

Marcus: We must have tolerance or there is no reason for our existence, my friend.

Crimins: Friend?

Karl: We're all friends here, Crimins.

Gripping the espresso group tightly, Paul nods.

Crimins: When's the last time any of you had me over for chicken and dumplings?

Karl: Put the gun down, and I'm sure Paul would make you a cup of coffee.

Paul nods, eagerly.

Crimins: I don't want *Paul* to make me a cup of coffee.

Terry: If you put down the gun, I'll get you a bottle of wine.

Crimins: I don't want your wine. I told you *a day of reckoning* was coming. Did you listen? And for this I was cast out, for a brotherhood of liars and a lie of brotherhood.

He takes aim at Paul, who shuts his eyes.

Marcus: Don't do this, my son.

Crimins: Son? You're next, old man.

Paul cringes as Crimins puts the gun to his head.

Marcus: Kill me first!

Karl: Watch what you're saying, Marcus. He's not fooling.

Marcus: I'm not fooling either. I have no wife, no family. I cannot bear witness anymore. Shoot me first, Crimins. *Please.*

Crimins: Don't tell me what to do.

Marcus: I'm not *telling* you what to do. I'm making a *last request.*

Crimins: I don't care about your request. I'm executing the homosexual chinaman *first*.

Karl: If you're killing people because they're gay, Crimins, save a round for me.

Dean: You're gay, Karl? But you have a daughter.

Karl: So?

Dean: And an ex-wife.

Karl: Maybe that's why it didn't work out.

Terry: This is a strange time to come out of the closet.

Karl: I've been out for years.

Dean: Not to us.

Paul: He told me.

Terry: And they say there's no gay conspiracy.

Karl: My private life is nobody's business. And I don't define myself by how I achieve orgasm.

Dean: Do you believe in gay marriage?

Karl: Is this San Francisco?

Crimins: *(frustrated)* Look, this is the killing order: the homosexual chinaman, then the Heeb, then the closeted faggot. *Maybe.*

Dean: What about me?

Crimins: What about you?

Dean: My father was agnostic, my mother was Catholic. I was baptized but never confirmed. I believe in God, but I'd like to be a Buddhist. I go to the Zen center but have a hard time meditating. I think I have A.D.D., but I can never sit still long enough to finish the test on the internet.

Crimins: Are you queer?

Dean: No.

Crimins: We'll talk later.

Again, Crimins takes aim at Paul, who raises his hands.

Marcus: Crimins! Shoot me first! My people were killed in the camps in Germany. Exterminated. I am a Jew. I've been prepared for this inevitability. Somewhat.

Terry: You know, fuck you, Marcus. Fuck you and *the Jews* - your self-prophesizing inevitability.

Karl: Terry, you're not helping.

Terry: I don't give a shit. Crimins is right.

Crimins: Welcome to the party, boy.

Terry: I don't know about Paul. He makes good espresso. As long as he doesn't queer off on me, I'm fine with it. You too, Karl. But Marcus has it coming.

Karl: You don't know what you're saying. That's completely anti-Semitic.

Terry: God forbid.

Dean: But he didn't do anything.

Terry: Yeah? Well then, who did? Who's going to take responsibility for all this? The republicans? The democrats? Foreigners? Terrorists? I say Marcus did it. And we string him up.

Karl: You can't be serious?

Crimins: Hanging's a good idea. I like a lynching.

Terry: We hang him right outside, as an example.

Karl: Of what?

Terry: Of people like *him.*

Marcus: It would not be a first time.

Crimins: Anybody got a camera? This will make a good picture.

Karl: This is madness.

Terry: Marcus defined himself first and foremost as a *Jew,* culturally and religiously. Not as an American, not a *World Citizen.* Crimins is right. Look where that kind of tribal stance has gotten us? He's not on *our team.* Look at the problems the Middle East brought us.

Karl: Or we brought them.

Dean: Nobody knows who dropped the first bombs. Or where the small pox came from. It could have been China, Pakistan, Korea, Syria...

Karl: Us.

Marcus: Let me say this, I am a *Jew*, but for years, I have not been pro-Israel. I am for a Jewish homeland. But I am more so for human rights. I am for a true democratic state, for all people. I am for the Bill of Rights. I *am* an American. History has made me into more of a Jew than I ever cared to be. But still, kill me... I'm ready... Shoot.

Terry: We should hang him. If people hear gunshots, they'll come running.

Crimins: Nobody's gonna come running. These days, you hear gunshots, you just pull the curtains tighter.

Terry: Let's not take a chance.

Crimins: I don't know.

Terry: Remember the Media? The Jew run media?

Crimins scowls.

Karl: What's got into you, Terry?

Terry: Shut up, Karl! *(to Crimins)* Remember Steven Spielberg and Michael Eisner? Remember *Seinfeld*? Or when they canceled *CSI: Miami*?

Crimins: All right, goddamn it! I get it. We'll kill him. Quietly.

He lowers the gun. Paul lowers his hands.

Don't worry, you'll get yours, Miss Saigon.

Terry steps in between Crimins and Paul.

Terry: Paul. Is that rope we used for the Cinco de Mayo piñata still in the storage room?

Paul: I think so.

Terry: Get it.

Paul: I'm not going to be a part of this.

Crimins: You don't have a choice.

Paul looks at Crimins, who waves him away with the gun.

You got sixty seconds to find that rope or I'll come back there blasting. Chop chop.

Paul looks hatefully at Crimins.

You can relieve yourself of that chunk of steel, too.

Paul sets down the espresso group, then stalks off stage to the storage room. Crimins moves to keep on eye on him.

Karl: I don't believe this.

Marcus: You've lived long enough that nothing should surprise you.

Crimins: *(to Marcus)* You come here. *(to Karl)* And you set back down. *(to Dean)* And you don't get any ideas.

Dean: I won't.

The payphone rings. Karl instinctively stands to answer it.

Crimins: *(points gun at Karl)* Uh-uh. Let it ring.

Karl sits back down, eyeing the payphone.

(sings in twangy voice) "Nobody knows I'm hurting, and nobody cares. Nobody knows I'm yearning, no one's aware. I've been livin' with more heartache than my share. But nobody's cryin' for meeeee..."

Karl: *(angrily to Terry)* Why aren't you accompanying him?

Terry: I don't take requests.

The payphone stops ringing – Karl grimaces.

Paul returns, carrying a length of rope with a brightly colored piñata attached to the end of it.

Crimins: Well, isn't that festive?

Dean: The café was covered with them. We had a mariachi band over there, and chips and salsa. We were drinking... what was that drink called again?

Paul: Café correcto.

Dean: That's right, café correcto. Coffee and tequila. They were good. You should have been here.

Crimins: I *should* have been here. But I wasn't invited.

Terry: All you missed was a hangover. I had seven of those correctos... *(to Karl and Dean)* Now *that's* drinking. I was up all night, puking.

Crimins: Serves you right, celebrating another country's Independence Day. You think they drink Budweiser on the Fourth of July in Mazatlan?

Dean: I had Thanksgiving in Tijuana once. Before the wall. We ate turkey tamales.

Crimins: Were you drinkin'?

Dean: Beer.

Crimins: That ain't drinkin'. It's certainly isn't any excuse to eat a damn turkey tamale.

Dean: Drinking beer is too drinking. Beer, wine, tequila. A drink is a drink if it is an alcoholic beverage.

Terry: Drinking wine is not drinking.

Crimins: Drinking beer is not drinkin'.

Dean: Is too.

Crimins: No it ain't. Unless you're queer.

Karl: This is insulting.

Crimins: Now you know how I feel, having to listen to you liberal crumb-bums. *You* offend *me*. But who's taking orders now?

Marcus: Cinco de Mayo is not Independence Day for Mexico.

Crimins: What?

Marcus: I said Cinco de Mayo is not Independence Day for Mexico. It commemorates the Mexican army's victory over the French at the Battle of Puebla in 1862.

Crimins: The hell it does.

Marcus: Some historians say the Battle of Puebla enabled the United States to finish with our Civil War and amass the military power to prevent Napoleon III and the French from conquering us.

Dean: The French were going to conquer us?

Crimins: My ass!

Dean: Then why were we drinking café correctos?

Marcus: Café correctos are a mixture of espresso and brandy topped with whipped cream.

Paul: Maybe it was Mexican coffee? Or is it café mexicano?

Marcus: There is a café mexicano and a Mexican coffee, but they are both made with Kaluha, not tequila.

Dean: But we called them *café correctos.*

Marcus shrugs.

Crimins: Don't listen to him. He's a goddamned liar.

Dean: At least we got the piñatas right.

Marcus: Piñatas originated in Italy. The Spanish adopted them from the Italians, and then, much later, they were *introduced* into Mexican culture.

Crimins: That's just plain crazy talk.

Dean: So, they are *Mexican.*

Marcus: If you consider hot dogs American.

Terry: Frankfurters?

Crimins: That's enough! Ask him how many died in the *supposed* Holocaust. He'll come up with a number. You and your revisionist Jew history. *(to Terry)* Give 'em enough rope.

Paul hands Terry the rope and the piñata. Terry unties the rope from the piñata. He offers the piñata to Karl to hold.

Karl: No way.

Terry hands the piñata to Dean, who shakes it.

Dean: There's still candy in it

Dean turns the piñata around looking for an opening.

There's no hole.

Terry: That's why it's called a piñata, Dean. That's why you hit it with a stick.

Dean sets the piñata on a table. He walks to the window and grabs a broom handle from the windowpane, set there to keep the window from sliding open.

Dean returns to the piñata. After sizing it up, he stikes the piñata viciously, again and again, smashing it to pieces while candy and paper mache go flying.

Crimins: Jesus H. Christ!

Dean: Hey, look. Kisses.

Crimins: Put down that stick!

Dean looks at the stick and then at Crimins holding the gun, and then at the candy on the floor again.

Dean: And Toffee Fay.

Crimins: It could be a trap.

Terry: Set by who? Dentists?

Karl reaches down and picks up a Kiss. He passes the wand of the Geiger counter over it. He unwraps the Kiss and pops it in his mouth.

Karl: Mmmm.

Terry: Gimme one.

Marcus: I'll miss chocolate.

Paul: I'm not cleaning up that mess.

Crimins: You'll do as I say. C'mon now. Shows over. Baby Huey found the chocolate center. Tie that noose.

Terry: I don't know how to tie a noose.

Crimins: This is what happens when you let homos infiltrate the boy scouts. A grown man can't tie a noose.

Paul: Nobody's safe.

Marcus: There is also a scaffold knot and a gallows knot...

Terry: But I wasn't an eagle scout and I'm not from Mississippi. Here, you tie it.

He attempts to hand the rope to Marcus.

Karl: His own noose?

Terry: What are you worried about, Geneva Conventions? We're living post-Abu Ghraib. Post ISIS info-purge... Anything goes.

Crimins: Give it here. *(grabs rope from Terry)* Take this. *(hands Terry the gun)* Keep 'em covered.

He coughs, clearing his throat, then speaks like a cross between someone in an "instructional video" and a salesman on an "infomercial," while making the noose.

The Hangman's Noose. To start you make an "N"-shape of the rope with plenty of extra rope off the bottom of the "N."

"What are you worried about, Geneva Conventions?"

Never mind the direction of the "N," keep wrapping tight coils spiraling up the outside, and then tuck the end of the rope through the top eye. Pull down the bottom eye to form the loop, then trap the tucked end of rope... *Voila!*

He looks up to see Terry pointing the gun at him.

These days, you can't trust anyone.

Terry: Shut up, before we stick your neck in that thing.

Karl: You had me going there for a minute, Terry.

Dean: Me too.

Terry: Just because I hate Barbra Streisand, it doesn't make me an anti-Semite. Or a homophobe.

Marcus: Thank you.

Paul: Yeah, thank you.

Terry: No problem. Buy me a coffee sometime. Now tie him to a chair so he's not dangerous.

Marcus: As long as he's breathing, he is going to be dangerous.

Terry: *(offers Marcus the gun)* Be my guest.

Reluctantly, Marcus takes the gun from Terry. Then with a surprising amount of agility, Marcus cocks the gun and points it at Crimins.

Crimins: Go ahead. I don't mind dying.

Marcus holds the gun to Crimins's head.

Do it, you fuckin' Jew!

Marcus's arm trembles. He lowers the weapon.

Marcus: I am not a murderer.

Karl puts his hand to Marcus's shoulder.

Karl: None of us are.

Crimins: You're a bunch of pussies.

Dean: "The meek shall inherit the earth."

Crimins: *The meek.* Not a bunch of pussies.

Paul and Dean tie Crimins to a chair set on the stage.

Go ahead, you can have the earth. It ain't worth shit now, anyway.

Karl leads Marcus to his chair. Paul and Dean fit the noose around Crimins' neck – his hands tied behind him.

Paul: That ought to hold him.

Crimins: Suddenly, you're a knot expert?

Paul: I've tied up a few men in my day.

He winks, and Crimins grimaces.

Karl: *(to Marcus)* Are you okay?

Marcus: *(shakily, puts on jacket)* I'll be fine when I get upstairs.

Paul: Why don't you stay? I'll make you a coffee?

Marcus: Save the coffee for yourselves. I've had enough.

Dean: But you haven't had any.

Trembling, Marcus steps toward the door.

Terry: See what happens when you just *smell* the coffee?

Paul: If you want to come with my family through the blue zone, you are more than welcome, Marcus. Everybody can come. Except you, Crimins.

Crimins: My heart is broke.

Terry: I have to wait for Theresa.

Paul: Maybe she'll want to go.

Terry: A death march isn't her style. She doesn't even like camping.

Dean: Maybe she won't come.

Terry glares at Dean.

I'm just saying. Brown zones are no place for women. After the Rape of Vallejo...

Karl: If she even exists.

Terry: What the fuck does that mean? *(scowls)* Both of you, shut the fuck up.

Marcus: *(opens the café door)* Thank you all for extending kindness in the face of this catastrophe. Humanity is still well represented. *(to himself)* "I've got a date on Market Street."

He closes the door behind him.

Crimins: Careful of them bathrooms with no showerheads!

Paul slaps Crimins across the back of his head.

Dean: What's going to happen to Crimins when we leave?

Karl: I'll watch him.

Dean: Don't you want to go to Southern Alberta, Karl, to see if your daughter's there?

Karl: *(looks at payphone)* I'm going to wait.

Terry: Hey, where's the gun?

Crimins: You better find it. There ain't a man in this room can take me *hand-to-hand*.

Terry: Marcus must have it. He's just upstairs, right?

Karl: Second floor. Third door on the right.

Terry: I'll find him. If Theresa comes, tell her...

A loud gunshot is fired from directly above the café, followed by the sound of a body falling to the floor.

The men look up at the ceiling.

BLACKOUT.

ACT TWO

Cafe Dante. The near future. Later.

Karl and Dean sip coffee at the table near the front window. Behind them, in the eerie outside glow, is the silhouette of Crimins's body hanging from a lamppost.

On the opposite window, in large dripping letters, the word "Imagine" is written in blood.

Paul is behind the counter, fumbling with the espresso machine. Terry tries to light a cigarette with unsteady hands. On the table near him is Crimins' survivalist gear and a coffee cup. On the floor are scattered candies, the burst piñata, and smashed guitar.

Between Terry and the seated men is a wide smear of blood, leading to the door. Their clothes are bloodstained.

Terry: Fuckin' piece of shit! *(flicks the lighter again)* God damn! Jesus fuck!

Karl breaks from his trance to look at Terry.

Karl: Do you have to swear *all* the time?

Terry: Yes, I do. If possible, *all* the time. Shit fuck piss. Fluent American.

Karl: Well, it's not helping.

Terry: Helping? What, *to light my cigarette*? No, Karl, it's not helping. But it is helping me to *communicate* that I am upset. That the day is not going as I had planned. I'm sorry to offend your suddenly delicate sensibilities, but fuck you.

The shadow of a person pushing a shopping cart strolls up to the hanging body.

Everybody curses.

The Shadow Person contemplates the body for a moment, then begins to unlace and take off Crimins's boots.

I'll tell you this, motherfucker is a word that will last. Hunky-dory, kittywampus? What the fuck is that? Almost useless. Cushion-cuffer? Shit, I went to church. I was an altar boy. You want to talk about archaic, grab a bible; concubine, chaste. *Probity.* The whole fuckin' thing. Obsolete.

The Shadow Person tosses one of Crimins's boots into the cart.

Motherfucker is there for us, building momentum.

The Shadow Person tosses Crimins's other boot into the cart.

It might be the *last word* the *last man* says with his *last breath.*

The Shadow Person pushes the cart away, out of sight – leaving Crimins swaying on the rope, shoeless.

Say it with me. *Motherfucker!*

The men are silent.

Paul: *(more to himself)* I was an altar boy.

Terry: Just because you spent time on your knees, doesn't make you an altar boy.

Paul: You pray to your god, I'll pray to mine.

Terry sparks the lighter.

Dean: Paul said there's no smoking in here.

Terry: And you're his echo?

Dean: No. But...

Terry: Did the Altar Boy say that *before or after* he smashed Crimins in the head with an espresso group?

Dean: He said...

Terry: *Before* or *after* we strung Crimins up on a lamppost with a piñata rope?

Dean: Paul said...

Terry: I don't give a shit what Paul said!

He lights his cigarette.

Karl: We've become a mob.

Dean: We should still have some rules.

Terry: We do. Mob rules.

Dean: Are we enough people to be a mob?

Terry: Let's see, there's two pints in a quart, twelve ounces of Diet Coke in a can. Gee, I don't know, Dean. Why don't you go ask Marcus?

Dean looks up at the ceiling.

Paul: I don't care if Terry smokes.

Terry looks at Dean and takes a big pull from the cigarette.

Dean: What about the rules?

Paul: We can bend them.

Dean: But no smoking isn't even a rule, it's a law.

Terry: Sue me in the World Court.

Terry exhales smoke towards Dean, who turns to Karl.

Dean: When you went upstairs... are you sure Marcus was dead?

Karl: Go see for yourself.

Terry: Check on Crimins while you're at it. Maybe he's playing possum.

Dean looks at the silhouette of Crimins hanging from the lamppost.

Paul walks around the counter toward Dean and Karl, stopping at the blood smear.

Paul: We should clean that up.

Terry: We?

Paul steps over the blood smear and sits down at the table.

Karl: It's disgusting.

Terry: And a dead body hanging outside isn't?

Karl: We're not outside.

Terry: What's the difference? A doorknob and a pane of glass?

Paul: Attitude and expectation.

Dean: Maybe we should cut Crimins down?

Terry: We already did, in the prime of his life.

Paul: Crimins didn't have a prime.

Terry: You mean the best was yet to come? *(looks towards Crimins)* That poor little daisy.

Karl: *(shoots Terry a glance)* Outside may be up for grabs, but *inside...* This is still a café.

Dean: With broken rules.

Paul: Bent.

Terry: Mob.

Dean: So if the café is still open and "with electricity comes responsibility..."

Terry: Dean, you say that again, I'll put this cigarette out in your eye.

Karl: Take it easy, Terry.

Terry: Take it easy? I don't think now is the time for *taking it easy*. For bumper sticker advice. Especially coming from someone with blood on their hands.

Karl looks at his hands – wiping them off on his pants.

Why not "One nuclear bomb can ruin your whole day." "Ass, grass, or gas. Nobody rides for free." That'll work. Everyone heading to the safety zones in their SUVs. Except for shit mileage, their four-wheel drives finally coming in handy. The SUVs weren't for the kids' soccer equipment, they were for traction over the dead bodies.

Terry sits down at the table with Crimins' survivalist gear.

Karl: We need to stay calm.

Terry: Maybe we should all switch to decaf?

Paul: Give us a break, Terry.

Terry: Well, "Take it easy." "Stay calm?" Thanks for the paternal advice, Karl, but that's what they said before letting loose the *peacekeeping* missiles. Starting a fuckin' free-for-all. "Stay fuckin' calm." All right, where did I leave my *knitting*?

Dean: They don't know who launched the first missile.

Terry: Yes, *they* do, you fuckin' lemming! You might not have a clue. We may not know who did what where when why, although I got some ideas on the subject, give or take an atrocity. But *they* most certainly do know who started it.

Paul: Terry's become a hippie.

"Maybe we should all switch to decaf?"

Terry picks up a knife from the pile of Crimins' gear.

Terry: Say that again. *(waves knife at Paul)* I can take a lot of shit, but you call me a hippie again, I'll cut your fuckin' throat.

Karl: Quit it! *(slams fist on the table)* What's been done has been done! Are we going to kill each other too?

Terry: I don't know. Maybe.

Karl: Well, I don't want to die. All right? *I don't want to die!*

Terry: *(sets down knife)* In the 21st century, it's a vicious thing to call someone a hippie.

Karl takes a napkin and wipes a spot of blood off his cheek.

Karl: We should try to clean up this mess as best we can. At least *inside.* *(points to blood on floor)* We shouldn't have to look at that while we're drinking our coffee.

Terry: You should have thought about that before you painted Beatles' lyrics on the window with Crimins's blood.

Dean: John Lennon.

Terry: What?

Dean: *John Lennon.*

Terry: John Lennon *was* a Beatle.

Dean: But he didn't write "Imagine" as a Beatle. He composed it solo.

Terry: *Compose?* That's a lofty word for scribbling a pop song. And what are you, the ghost of Marcus? I say, once a Beatle always a Beatle. All the good ones are dead anyway.

Paul: Yoko's dead too.

Terry: This shit cloud's only silver lining.

Dean: Before the signal went down, I saw Ringo on TV in a "Rock for Nuclear Relief" concert.

Karl: Can't something bad happen without people having a rock concert? When did that become our sum total response to tragedy?

Dean: What's wrong with Ringo singing at a benefit?

Terry: He was singing?

Dean: "Let it Be."

Terry: That fucker. Did he do *"Octopus's Garden"* too?

Dean: No. Just "Let it Be."

Paul: Ever notice Ringo's songs all have underwater themes, "Octopus's Garden," "The Yellow Submarine?"

Terry: You mean his *compositions?* Ever notice Ringo's usually *stoned*, i.e. "under the sea," i.e. "in an octopus's garden."

Dean: It's hard to tell with the sunglasses he wears.

Terry: You mean when he's "in the shade?" The walrus may have been Paul, but Ringo's definitely one under-the-sea in-the-fuckin'-shade octopus.

Dean: I don't think that's what the song's about.

Terry: What? Like "Puff the Magic Dragon" is just a children's song?

Karl: Will you please stop quibbling! I've never heard such moronic banter.

Terry: Hey, rumor has it this is still a café. You want *normal*, you get moronic banter. You don't like it, drink your coffee somewhere else.

Karl: After everything that's happened, you're blathering about Yoko.

Terry: She broke up the Beatles, Karl!

Karl crumples his napkin.

Instead of talking, would you rather I dip my finger in Crimins' busted head and write the word "Revolution" in the other window? How about "Hey, Jude?"

Karl: Look, I admit it, I lost it there for a while. With Crimins. With the blood on the window. After Marcus. We all lost it. Okay? But here we are *now*. And I'd like to enjoy this cup of coffee *now*, whether it kills me or not.

Karl sets down his crumpled napkin, then sips his coffee.

Dean: I'm with you, Karl. Can you please pass me a napkin?

Karl reaches for a napkin from the dispenser.

Karl: Sure, Dean. Here's a napkin.

Karl hands Dean a napkin. Dean dabs the edges of his mouth, then at blood on his hand.

Dean: Thanks.

Karl: You're welcome. My pleasure.

Dean crumples the napkin, looking for some place to toss it.

Paul: I'll take it. I have to put out the trash anyway.

Paul walks around the counter, then drags out a plastic garbage can on wheels.

Terry: An act of futility.

Paul drags the garbage can across the blood-smeared floor to the front door.

There aren't garbage men anymore, Paul.

Paul: This is still part of my job.

Paul opens the door, dragging the can out by Crimins's body. He steps back into the café.

I'm going to do what I'm supposed to do. I can't control other people. They can decide for themselves if they want to take care of their end of the bargain.

Terry: Their end-of-the-world bargain?

Paul: "With electricity, comes responsibility."

Terry takes a big drag on his cigarette, then pantomimes extinguishing it in Paul's eye.

Karl: We all have a responsibility, with or without electricity. To make things as normal as possible.

Terry: I don't see anybody paying for their coffee. What about that? Are we playing tea party? We've got moronic banter. Maybe someone should pay for their fuckin' coffee?

Paul: The café's become non-profit.

Dean: Can you do that?

Paul: *(sits down)* Just did.

Terry: Then who's cleaning up the blood? You're wearing the apron, *comrade.*

Paul: *(takes off apron)* My shift's over.

Terry laughs, as if he has won a small victory.

Dean: So, the café's closed?

Paul: I finished my shift. I put out the garbage, someone else can mop up the blood.

Dean: Maybe this *could* become a co-op or something? *Profit sharing.*

Terry: You clean up Crimins' blood, I'll put a buck in the tip jar.

Paul: I'll give you the keys to the place.

Dean: Really?

Paul: You can have them. After I finish my coffee, I'm loading up on beans and heading north.

Dean: No joke?

Terry: There's no sense in having a business, Dean. Money is irrelevant. Paul's got the right idea. Coffee beans are more valuable than diamonds.

Dean: I don't think so.

Terry: That's what you get for thinking. You'd be better off with a roll of toilet paper than a roll of twenties. In a few days, if not a few hours, people will be giving away their entire bank accounts for a breath of fresh air.

Karl: Don't listen to him, Dean. Go ahead, take the keys.

Paul fishes out keys from his pocket. He tosses them to Dean.

It's important that this remains a café, that there is a sanctuary of order and protocol somewhere in the world. If money is worthless, Dean can create a barter system.

Dean: And when things get back to normal, it will be the people that held onto the businesses, the money and real estate, who'll come out ahead. It's an opportunity.

Terry: That's dark, man. Real dark. And call me a pessimist, but things are never going to get *back to normal*. We were lucky to have our day.

Dean: A day is a lifetime for a butterfly.

Terry: But you're no Monarch.

Paul: Monarch butterflies live longer than a day.

Karl: Species adapt.

Paul: *(sings David Bowie lyric)* "Ch-ch-ch changes."

Karl: When was *normal*, anyway?

Terry: When you didn't have to think about the destruction of the planet first thing in the morning.

Paul: Before terrorists started carrying nuclear bombs in briefcases.

Dean: When you could get a newspaper and watch TV?

Terry: *(points outside)* When that fuckin' glow wasn't outside.

Karl: The sun has always been zooming in. We've been living with that knowledge for a long time. The inevitable destruction of our planet. Our own death.

Dean: Isn't that why we were trying to go to Mars?

Terry: That's right, Dean. So we could have a new place to flip mad-cow burgers and build prisons.

Paul: Who's being dark now?

Dean: They said they found traces of life on Mars.

71

Terry: Yeah. Water and excrement. Same thing they're gonna find here.

The payphone rings, startling the men. Karl stands to answer it, but the telephone only rings once.

Dean: Who do you think is trying to call?

Karl sits back down.

An emergency siren blares. The message plays over the PA system: "Crisis code black. Terror alert red. Carry district ID at all times. Only authorized personnel may cross into colored sectors. Stay in your home zone. Report any terrorist activity to police immediately, including suspicious behavior and unauthorized travel. We will not be defeated. Our spirit is indomitable."

What's indomitable?

Terry: Your stupidity. *(stamps out cigerette)* I'll tell you when normal was. Normal was high school. I had a girlfriend, a fake ID. Parents that put food on the table.

A drip falls from the ceiling, splattering on the floor to the left of the counter.

Paul: High school was not my normal. It was more like an unfortunate, temporary state of mind.

Dean: Kids picked on me.

Paul: Tell me about it.

Terry: *(sarcastic)* You two got picked on?

Another drip falls from the ceiling, splattering on the floor. The men see it, and look up to see more drops fall.

Shit no.

Dean walks over to the splatter on the floor.

Dean: It's blood.

Another drop hits Dean on the head – he jumps back as if he's been bitten. He feels the top of his head, and then holds out two fingers smeared with blood.

(looks at ceiling) That's Marcus's room.

Terry: You should work for Google maps.

Karl: I don't know if I'm going to make it.

Dean goes behind the counter and grabs a towel – wiping his head and fingers.

Coming back around the counter with the towel and a coffee cup, he cleans the blood off the floor. He positions the coffee cup beneath the drip. A drop falls into the cup.

Dean peers inside at the blood – then sets the cup back on the floor to catch more blood.

Dean: I'll clean the rest up later.

Dean tosses the bloody towel on the counter.

Terry: Maybe somebody should check on Marcus again?

Roll him over or something? *(nobody responds)* Fine. I don't give a fuck.

Another drop of blood falls.

Dean: We might need a bigger cup.

Terry: And a Band-Aid.

Paul: Probably a new ceiling. This place was built back when they didn't care how things were built.

Terry: You mean the 20th century? *(points to the leak)* It's a tough way to find out you got thin walls.

Paul: We have leaks all the time.

Dean: From Karl's sink?

Paul: Sinks, toilets, showers. All the pipes back up.

Dean: Who owns this place?

Paul: Erik Weiss. You know, the guy that wore those ratty sports coats? Came in late afternoons.

Terry: The old man with the nose and the haircut. The pants? The *slacks?*

Paul nods.

I thought he was homeless.

Paul: Far from it. But he was in Seattle.

"We might need a bigger cup."

The men all shake their heads.

He went to check on the competition.

Terry: Bad idea.

Dean: He owned the hotel? The SRO?

Paul: The whole building.

Terry: The homeless guy?

Paul: *(to Terry)* You should have seen his girlfriend.

Terry: The homeless guy?

Paul: He wasn't homeless, Terry. Do you listen?

Terry: I'm saying, you look like that, it's only a matter of time. A self-fulfilling prophesy. Like Crimins with his combat gear. Eventually, you're at war.

Terry pushes the canteen in Crimins' pile of belongings.

Paul: You would have liked his girlfriend. *(indicates large breasts)* But she went to Seattle too.

Dean: What kind of car?

Paul: A Jaguar.

Dean: Was it an XKR?

Paul: Yep.

Dean: Was it black? I think I remember seeing a black Jag.

Terry: Who cares about his fuckin' car?

Dean: Who cares about his girlfriend? Supposedly you've got Theresa.

Terry: Supposedly? Fuck you, supposedly. But I can still look. The impulse for sex hasn't been beaten out of me just because I've got a girlfriend.

Karl: Give it time.

Terry: Plus, we have an understanding.

Dean: She let's you sleep with other women?

Terry: No. But I can look at women when she's not around.

Karl: A relationship based on trust. Just like me and my ex-wife.

Terry: No, Karl, that was a farce not a relationship. And gay men can always look at women. Nobody gives a shit.

Karl: My wife and I had a relationship. We were married. We had a daughter. What we didn't have for the last five years was sex.

Terry: At least not with each other.

Karl's expression acknowledges that Terry is correct.

Dean: What year was the Jag?

Terry: Will you shut up about the car?

Dean: You're talking about a dead woman.

Terry: So? Marilyn Monroe's dead. People still talk about her. That porn star that died from the overdose... people still jack-off to her. Fuck, everybody's dead. No more Hollywood. How do you like your Botox and liposuction now? Being on the A list? Still, if you said Scarlett Johansson, I'd get lumber.

Paul: You'd get lumber if I said Porky Pig.

Terry: That's because you'd be pursing your lips.

Paul blows Terry a kiss.

Karl: They're both cartoons. Half that woman's body wasn't real.

Terry: What do you mean? Fake tits are real. You touch them, there they are. They're not holograms. Your hand doesn't pass through them.

Karl: They're unnatural.

Terry: How many fake tits you ever felt up, Karl?

Karl: I like natural bodies. No other comment.

Terry: Too bad for you. But I wouldn't kick Scarlett out of bed for eating toxic crackers or having gone to the plastic surgeon.

Paul: Terry's having a Viagra flashback.

Terry: You ever do Viagra and ecstasy?

Paul: *Sextasy?* I've been known to disco.

Karl: High with a constant erection is no way to go through life.

Terry: There's a better way?

Karl: What ever happened to just smoking a little pot?

Terry: You end up in a sexless marriage with a member of the wrong sex.

Karl: A couple of tokes from a joint?

Terry: You're dating yourself, Karl. Drugs need to match the tragedy of the day. That's why we've evolved from wine to crack.

Paul: To proscribed designer drugs.

Dean: So, if Weiss is gone, somebody *could* take over the café?

Paul: You've got the keys.

Dean: I always wanted a Jag.

Terry: Go find it. It's probably at the airport. Long term parking.

Dean: You think?

Terry: You're dumber than I thought.

Karl: Weiss would probably be happy if someone was taking care of his car. And the café.

Terry: Weiss would be happy to be alive, driving his car. Fuckin' his girlfriend. Forget the café.

Dean: But he went to Seattle.

Paul: Most everyone's dead anyway.

Terry: But what if they're not? It doesn't matter because Dean's thieving takes place outside the café? Now we only care about what happens, scratch that, what it *looks like* inside. We can kill Crimins as long as we clean up, neat and tidy? Put out the trash cans. Catch the dripping blood.

Karl: It's easy to poke holes in things, Terry.

Terry: Ideas and flesh, first and foremost.

Karl: We're trying to make the best of a bad situation.

Terry: That's an understatement.

Dean: Everybody's taking the SUVs anyway, not the sports cars.

Paul: You could be shot as a looter.

Another shadow appears in the window, looming outside.

Dean: The airport's a good idea. They've probably got a lot of awesome cars. Porsches, BMWs, maybe a convertible 65 Mustang. I could put them in the garage at my apartment. Nobody else lives there anymore. It's secure.

Terry: Perfect. What do you want with you when you die? A Jag, a Beemer, a Porsche, and a '65 Mustang. Vroom vroom. Way to go American at the end, Dean. It would have been sad if you wanted nothing from your own country.

Dean: I'm not hurting anyone.

Terry: You're hurting me, buddy. *(taps his chest)* Right here.

There is a knock on the door. The men turn to see the looming shadow. Terry grabs Crimins' knife from the table.

(in a high-pitched voice) Who is it?

*The door opens and **Randy** (30s), black, cautiously steps halfway into the café. He is holding something behind his back. He speaks with an African accent.*

Randy: Is the café open?

Dean: Yes.

Terry: No.

Dean: Is too. Under new management.

Randy: *(confused)* Are you hanging white people?

Terry: We are white people. *(looks at Paul)* Most of us.

Randy: I thought you might be hanging white people.

Terry: We were. But just the one.

Dean: Not because he was white though.

Terry: Are you looking for a posse to hang white people with?

Randy: I'm a cab driver.

Karl: Nobody called a cab from here.

Terry: Unless you're driving to Canada.

Randy: *(points at Crimins)* What did he do?

Paul: He threatened us.

Karl: He was in the wrong place at the wrong time.

Dean: He started it.

Terry: He fucked around with the wrong motherfuckers.

Randy nods, then peers around the café. He has a gun behind his back - but the men don't see it.

Karl: *(indicates Crimins)* That was a mistake.

Randy's head disappears from the doorway, then reappears.

Randy: It doesn't look like a mistake.

Randy sees a drip of blood fall from the ceiling, the smear on the floor, and the blood-written "Imagine" on the window.

Are you a cult?

Dean: We're a café.

Terry: Trying to become a mob.

Randy: You been drinking the water? It gets in your system. The *radiation*.

Dean: We've only been drinking the coffee.

The men look at Randy who looks back at them, skeptically.

Karl: Come on in.

Paul checks his watch, then reaches for his apron.

Paul: I'll make you one, if you want? *(to Dean)* Right, boss?

Dean smiles, as Paul puts on his apron.

Terry: I thought your shift was done?

Paul: I'm putting in overtime. *(walks to counter)* Come watch me, Dean. To see how it's done.

Dean follows Paul.

Randy: *(indicates Terry)* Why do you have that knife? What are those candies doing on the floor? Why is that guitar smashed?

Terry: Turns out I knew one classic Who song.

Randy doesn't respond to Terry's joke.

Look, man, shit happens.

Randy nods in a noncommittal manner.

How's it *outside*? You got questions about how *all that happened*? By comparison we got it going on in here. Neat and tidy. That's the New Doctrine.

Karl gives Terry an annoyed look.

Randy: Where's Mr. Weiss?

Terry: The homeless guy?

Paul glares at Terry.

Paul: He went to Seattle.

Randy nods, sadly.

You must be part of the late afternoon crowd?

Randy nods again.

Don't worry, you'll love my coffee.

Dean: I read somewhere that the number two sexual fantasy for women, behind their *express mail* delivery person, is their coffee jock.

Paul: That's because we're sexy.

Terry: That's because caffeine's a drug and junkies love the pusherman.

Dean: I also read that women find men doing housework erotic. And that the most erotic *smell* for men is cinnamon buns.

Terry: No surprise there, huh, Dean?

Karl: Maybe the coffee jock fetish is a combination of those two elements?

Terry: Who says journalism is dead? Where are you getting this hard news? Back issues of *Cosmo*?

Paul: *(to Randy)* You want milk? Macchiato? Latte?

Sheepishly, Randy enters the café – cautiously letting the door shut behind him.

Randy: Latte, please.

The men spot Randy's gun. Terry brandishes the knife at Randy, as Karl holds up his hands.

Karl: Please! We've had enough blood for one day.

Randy looks from Karl to Terry. He holsters his gun, then steps over the blood smear.

Randy: Someone should clean that up.

Terry relaxes.

Terry: *(to Dean)* Hear that? The customer's always right.

Dean: Paul, do we have a mop?

Paul points back to the closet. Dean disappears, then returns wheeling a mop bucket. He starts to swab up the blood.

Randy moves to the farthest vacant table.

85

Karl: You can sit with us if you'd like.

Randy: This is my spot.

The shadow of a dog approaches. It stands on its hind legs, up against the window – pawing and licking at the blood.

Shoo!

Randy pounds the window, scaring off the dog.

I hate dogs.

Paul sets the coffee on the counter.

Paul: Here you go.

Randy walks to the counter, again stepping over the blood.

Randy: Thank you.

Paul: You're welcome.

Randy reaches for his wallet.

That's not necessary.

Dean: Yes it is. That's three bucks.

Randy pays, then puts a dollar in the tip jar. The register rings.

Thank you.

Randy reseats himself, as Dean smiles at the transaction.

Terry: Grinning like an idiot.

Dean resumes his mopping.

Karl: *(to Randy)* What's your name?

Randy: Randy.

Karl: I'm Karl. *(indicates the others)* This is Paul, Terry, Dean.

Randy nods hello, then unclips a Geiger counter from his belt. He checks his coffee.

Randy: How do you know it's good?

Paul: We checked it with a Geiger counter. Same as you.

Randy: Something else could be wrong with it. Other than radiation.

Dean: *(stops mopping)* But we drank it. We *all* drank it. And I can't sell bad coffee.

Terry: Of course you can. You know what the Chinese put in toothpaste?

Paul: It will be fine, Dean.

Terry: It may not be fine. But Marcus and Crimins were the only one's who didn't drink the coffee, and look at them. *(salutes with his cup)* Cheers.

Randy raises his cup, saluting as well. He takes a sip.

Randy: That's good coffee.

Karl: If you don't mind me asking, what kind of accent is that?

Randy: I'm from Mauritania.

Terry: You're shitting me.

Randy: You know where it is?

Dean: It's in North Western Africa. You claimed your independence from France. It's a wasteland.

Randy: It's my *home*land.

Dean: Sorry. That's just what I heard.

Randy: You heard wrong. There is much desert, but there are beautiful beaches too. And natural resources. We have iron...

Terry: Wow. *Iron.*

Randy: We had oil too. Today, Mauritania might be a better place to live than America.

Terry: You mean equally as bad.

Randy: *(eyes Terry)* Most people don't know where Mauritania is.

Terry: Most people don't give a fuck.

Randy: *Americans.*

Terry: No, *most* people.

Karl: *(to Randy)* I thought you looked familiar. I've been in your cab.

Terry: Okay, so I'm not totally crazy. This isn't some sort of run on Mauritania.

Karl: I have to admit, that's how I heard of Mauritania, Randy here told me.

Randy: That's how Americans learn their geography, from riding in cabs.

Dean: Maybe that's when things went wrong? When our schools got bad?

Terry: Try getting an education in Mauritania.

Randy: What do you know?

Terry: You don't recognize me? I was in your geology class. We studied iron together.

Dean mops near Terry, forcing him to lift his feet.

Karl: Well, you can't have a democracy without an educated populous.

Dean: Why's that?

Karl: Because you have to know what you're voting for, Dean.

Randy: You don't think uneducated people know the difference between right and wrong?

Karl: That's not what I'm saying.

Dean: Isn't that what we vote for, what's right and wrong? You don't have to know all the countries on a map to be a good person.

Karl: But you do have to be educated to cast your vote for the best choice, to enact what you think is right.

Terry: That's bullshit. It doesn't matter what *political* system you have, democracy, communism, dictatorship. Nobody votes for anything that matters. Keeping small pox around? Blowing Afghanistan back to the Dark Ages? Spying? Corporations are people? I don't remember any of that on a ballot.

Karl: This isn't a *direct* democracy.

Randy: It's a corporate oligarchy.

Terry: *Was.* That's the word here. And I don't care what it *was.* The problem is that humans can't build something without using it; bombs, chemicals, a fuckin' mousetrap.

Paul: You're not a hippie, Terry. You're a technophobe.

Terry: I'm telling you, it's human nature.

Randy: It's the *nature* of the First World.

Terry: First World, Third World, Fifth Dimension. It doesn't matter. They all do the same thing once they fill their stomachs and build the machinery.

Dean: I'd vote for Mauritania not to be starving.

Terry: Not me. I'm a heartless American. I'd vote for children with bloated bellies and fly-encrusted eyes.

Randy: *(to Terry)* I don't think I like you.

Terry: That's your problem.

Randy: Maybe.

Karl: Didn't you tell me in your cab that Mauritania still had a slave trade?

Randy looks uncomfortable. Terry laughs, saluting again with his cup.

Terry: To human nature!

Paul sits down with Karl.

Paul: Well, something went wrong.

Terry: You want to know when everything went to shit? When the world broke into a million pieces and couldn't be put back together again? I'll tell you. It was the death of Teddy Ballgame.

Dean: Who?

Karl: Ted Williams?

Paul: Who?

Randy: Ted Williams, Boston Red Sox. Last man in the majors to hit four hundred.

Terry: *(to Randy)* How'd you know?

Randy: I'm a cabbie. The games always on in the car.

Terry: Then you know how he did it?

Randy doesn't respond.

Last day of the season. Double-header. Teddy Ballgame was hitting four hundred, *technically.* .3996, *actually.* But you round up, so four hundred. Everybody said he should take the day off. The Yankees had already clinched the pennant, Boston was out of the race. Athletes today *(corrects himself)*, recent athletes, before there were no more fuckin' athletes, would have gladly sat out to protect their *accomplishment*, their shoe contracts. Not Teddy Ballgame. We're talking about a man who interrupted his career *twice*, once to enlist in WWII as a fighter pilot, and then to *re-enlist* for Korea. He damn-well fuckin-A was going to play in *both* games. And he went six-for-eight on the day with a home run. Hit a line drive so hard, he dented a speaker on the stadium p.a. system. Ended up hitting four-oh-six on the year.

Paul: So he was a baseball player?

Terry: He was the fuckin' greatest hitter of all-time!

Dean: When did he play?

Terry: He hit a home run in his last at-bat in 1960. And at his Hall-of-Fame induction, he said Satchel Page and Josh Gibson *(looks at Randy), Negro-leaguers*, should be honored in the Hall too.

Randy: They said he was an asshole.

Terry: He was a *class* act.

Karl: I thought he wouldn't sign autographs for kids?

Terry: Class act.

Randy: He spit on fans.

Terry: They fuckin' loved him.

Randy: They booed him.

Terry: Fuck you, Mauritania. Stick with Third World kickball or whatever you call soccer. What do you know about our national pastime?

Randy: Sports radio. Long time listener. Everybody knows Ted Williams was an asshole. Never won a World Series. DiMaggio was the best. Fifty-six game hitting streak. That's why he was the MVP in '41, not Williams.

Terry looks shocked.

Terry: That's propaganda. Joe never hit .400. And none of his teammates liked him, including his brothers.

Randy: Fifty-six straight, "The Streak."

Terry: Fuck "The Streak." A run of luck. What did he do for *Marilyn Monroe?* Nothing but heartbreak.

Paul: I've heard of Joe DiMaggio.

Terry: A pin-striped prick.

Randy: "A nation turns its lonely eyes to you."

Dean: I've heard that, too.

Terry: A folk song. It means nothing. Ted Williams was the gold standard. Not to mention a world-class fly fishermen.

Karl: Neither of you ever saw Williams or DiMaggio play.

Terry: I've seen *footage.* But I'm not talking strictly about what he did on the field.

Karl: So, you're saying, when Williams died, it was the end of an era.

Terry: No. But that's true. Because soon after his retirement, you see a shift in sports, from emphasizing the *team concept* to focusing on the *superstar*. And a parallel shift in this country from Protestantism and their work ethic to Catholicism's notion of the individual, Christ on the cross becoming more important than the cross itself, i.e., the *team sacrifice.* One man takes on the *entire* burden. And the more Catholic idea of God living in church. Hence, the home field advantage. Finally, it spins completely out of control, manifesting with Michael Jordan, a player who is bigger than the league he plays in. And Lebron, *King James,* the Savior of Clevelend.

Randy: You can't compare the NBA to Major League Baseball.

Karl: Or to religion.

Paul: Thank God I don't watch sports.

Dean: I liked the Super Bowl. Especially the half-time show.

Randy: Joltin' Joe was better. So were Willie Mays and Barry Bonds, even without the asterisk.

Terry: That's San Francisco sports talk radio bullshit!

Karl: He has a right to his opinion.

Terry: Not if it's wrong.

Paul: So, which of those things was the last straw, Terry?

Terry: None of them. They were just *indicators*. Everything could still have turned out okay. Sure it was the loss of a great man, the end of an era, like Karl said. But that happens at the end of every era. It's what happened *after* he died.

Karl: You mean when his son cryogenically froze his head?

Randy: They should have cloned Joe.

Terry: What the fuck is wrong with you, Mauritania?

Randy: I'm a Yankee's fan.

Terry: Because Steinbrenner best represented our *better self*?

Randy: When I came to this country, I lived in New York.

Terry: That's hardly a reason. And not what I'm talking about. Yeah, the Williams kid froze Ted's head. Then sold off his dad's DNA like a box of autographed balls. *Not* a classy move. But remember the guy with all the heads?

Dean: What guy with all the heads?

Terry: *The guy with all the heads.* The rich guy who was cloning all those heads and had a trophy room full of them like he was some kind of big game hunter.

Karl: Richard Allen Ellison.

Terry: Yep. Ellison's family invented pockets or something. Anytime somebody put something inside of something else, the Ellison family got like three cents.

Karl: It was a patent for a hermetic seal. And a *space hinge*, I think.

Dean: Like Stonehenge?

Terry: Yeah, Dean. Just like Stonehenge, only in space. You know how when you stick your head up your ass and time bends?

Karl: *Hinge.* Not henge.

Terry: Can I finish?

Paul: Are you in a hurry, Terry? You got somewhere to go?

Terry: Yeah, to the park. To lay in the grass and eat apples, look up at the shifting clouds and play Frisbee with my golden retriever.

Dean: You got a dog?

Terry: Am I wasting my fuckin' breath here?

Karl: Go ahead, finish.

Terry: So, Ellison had enough money to get weird, put Michael Jackson and Elvis to shame. And nobody knew about the heads. Not his wife, kids, friends. Not the UPS guy. Not his coffee jock...

Paul: Don't be too sure.

Terry: *Nobody.*

Dean: What did he do with them?

Terry: He *mounted* them. Decorated the walls of his secret office. Teddy Ballgame, Stalin, Paris Hilton. A Neanderthal man. Bill Clinton. He bought all this shit at auctions for the DNA: bones, locks of hair, Lewinsky's jacked-off on dress. Then he paid scientists from that Dolly the Lamb cult to make the trophy heads.

Karl: Apparently, he'd just sit in his office, look at the heads and drink Scotch.

Terry: Dewar's had a big jump in sales.

Paul: Like White Broncos after O.J.

Randy: O.J. was innocent.

Terry: So was Pol Pot.

Paul: Pol Pot said he died with a clean conscience.

Dean: I never heard about any of this.

Terry: It was right after Stonehenge.

Karl: So, that was it, huh? Cloning?

Randy: Messing with God's business.

Terry: No, not just cloning. But cloning *heads* of dead people to mount on your wall so you can sit and contemplate them while you're drinking Scotch.

Paul: There are cultures where people keep heads, especially conquered enemies. For spiritual reasons. Or to scare off warring tribes.

Terry: Did they clone them? Did they have one of Merv Griffin? Cher? Fuckin' Condoleezza Rice?

Dean: That would be a scary head.

Dean looks up to see if the drip has stopped, and then picks up the white coffee cup and sets it on the counter. He puts the mop bucket away.

Randy: One bad apple doesn't ruin the whole barrel.

Terry: Is that an old Mauritanian saying?

Dean: Does your country have apples?

Before Randy can answer, there is the rumble of a huge engine followed by the shadow of a tank slowly passing by.

After it is gone, there are screams and shouts, chanting and clanging, tambourines and drumbeats.

What is it?

The noise gets louder, approaching the café. Terry grabs Crimins' knife from the table. Dean grabs the piñata stick. Paul nods to the espresso machine, and Dean hands him an espresso group. Randy draws his gun.

Terry: *(to Randy)* You expecting friends?

Randy shakes his head.

Through the window are shadows of a band of Revelers, howling. They cut down Crimins from the lamp post.

I hope that's not his clan.

Randy: Klan?

The café door opens and the Revelers burst in holding Crimins, the piñata rope still around his neck.

The Revelers are a motley all-male crew in strange costumes. They wail and chant, each experiencing their own religious ecstasy as they march and dance around the café.

Reveler 1: We are the *Chosen*!

99

Reveler 1 sensuously wraps a scarf around Karl's neck.

Come with us. We are readying ourselves to welcome Him.

Reveler 2: He will be here soon.

Dean: Who?

Paul: *Him* who.

Dean: Him who who?

Terry: What are you guys, a fuckin' knock-knock joke?

Reveler 1: Our savior is returning.

Terry: I think I saw him. Blue eyes? Impossibly light skin for a Middle Easterner?

Reveler 2: He will smile upon us. And take us away.

Dean: Where?

Terry: East Oakland. In Randy's cab.

Randy: They're not getting in my cab.

Reveler 1: It has been prophesied.

Terry: Hard to argue with that, Randy. I hope you got a full tank.

Reveler 1: We must prepare ourselves. It is time.

Terry: *(indicates Crimins)* That's what *he* said.

Reveler 1 and Reveler 2 look at Terry gripping his knife. The Revelers mood turns foul.

Karl: We don't want any trouble.

Dean: Not in the café.

Reveler 1: We have come with a message of eternal love.

Randy: I don't think so.

Reveler 2: He is merciful.

Terry: Despite all the indications.

Reveler 1: Accept His love.

Reveler 1 takes a menacing step towards Randy, who points his gun at him.

Randy: I can accept your love from right there.

Reveler 1 pauses. The other Revelers watch tensely, waiting for orders.

Dean: *(to the Revelers)* Look, unless you're going to order something, I'm going to have to ask you all to leave.

The Revelers look at Dean, confused.

This is still a café. Under new ownership. Please excuse the mess.

One of the Revelers steps forward from the pack.

Reveler 3: Can I use the bathroom?

Dean: The bathroom is for customers only.

Reveler 3 returns to the group.

Reveler 1: It is His plan to destroy all of Earth's sinners. And to bring us Salvation.

Reveler 1 raises his right hand, making a peace sign.

Reveler 2: We will soon be delivered. If you do not accept His way, you will be left behind to suffer.

Dean: I'm just trying to run a business.

Reveler 1: We must all repent!

Reveler 2: Repent!

The Revelers stare at the café patrons, who stare back.

Reveler 1: The Judgment is upon us!

Reveler 1 tugs on Reveler 2's arm, then gestures for the group to leave.

The Revelers open the café door and begin to parade out, howling and singing again – taking Crimins' body with them.

Reveler 1 and Reveler 2 start to leave, but Reveler 1 stops halfway out the door and turns.

Randy points his gun at him.

Peace.

Dean sets down the piñata stick.

Dean: Peace.

Karl looks at Dean, then back at Reveler 1 in the doorway.

Karl: Peace.

Paul sets the metal espresso group onto the coffee counter.

Paul: Peace.

Randy slowly lowers his gun.

Randy: Peace.

They all turn to Terry, still holding his knife.

Terry: What the fuck do you want from me? I told you I'm not a hippie.

Karl: You can't even say the word.

Terry: They're religious nuts. Even without the religious part, they'd still be *nuts*.

Karl: You can't find it in your heart to wish them Peace?

Terry: I'm saving my wishes, Karl. For Theresa to get here. For another cup of coffee.

Reveler 1: You've got to feel His spirit. *(points at Terry)* You will feel His wrath.

They look at the shadows of the other Revelers dancing by the window, away from the café. Their chants and screams, fading.

"And the seventh angel poured out his vial into the air; and there came a great voice out of the temple of heaven, from the throne, saying, *It is done.*" Revelation 17.

Terry: "But the second mother was with the seventh son, And they were both out on Highway 61." Bob Dylan.

Reveler 1 scoffs, then makes the sign of the cross. He exits with Reveler 2.

Terry sighs and tosses the knife back onto the table.

Dean: Those were potential customers, Terry.

Terry: Sorry, Carnegie.

Another shadow appears in the window, approaching.

Terry quickly picks up his knife again. Randy aims his gun at the door.

If that freak's coming back as a suicide bomber...

*The café door opens, in steps **Theresa** (40) attractive, but older than expected.*

Theresa: Don't shoot!

Randy lowers his gun.

Pookie!

The men look at Terry.

Paul: Pookie?

Theresa embraces Terry, then looks around at the café.

Theresa: What's going on here?

The men all look embarrassed and guilty.

Terry: Karl, Paul, Dean. Randy. This is Theresa.

Everybody nods hello.

I thought you might not be coming.

Dean: I thought you didn't exist.

Theresa: I was running late and then waiting for that group of crazies to leave.

Paul: Which reminds me, I got to go. This sector closes in an hour.

Paul goes behind the counter to get a sack of coffee beans.

Dean: To Alberta?

Paul: If that's where it's safe.

Terry: It's not safe anywhere.

Dean: Some places are going to be safer than others.

Terry: Tell it to the dinosaurs.

Theresa: What are we going to do, Terry? I can't go back to the cellar. *(to Paul)* You're going to Canada?

Paul: I'm going to be with my family.

Terry: Too late for me.

Randy: Me too.

Paul: I told you, everyone can come.

Terry: I'm not ending my life with a whimper. Marcus had the right idea.

Theresa: Who's Marcus?

The men look up at the ceiling.

Paul: How about you Dean?

Dean: I'm going to stay here and run the café. It's my chance. When things clear up, you can come back and I'll make you coffee. On the house.

Terry: Are you joining the radiation parade to Canada, Karl?

Karl: I don't think so.

Paul: *(surveys café)* Funny, if we survive this catastrophe, we'll be nostalgic for this place. Our grandchildren won't understand. They'll just wonder why we hoard food or run a Geiger counter over our coffee, even after the world has cleansed itself.

Terry: You expecting grandchildren, Paul? (*to Dean*) You sure you don't want to go to Canada, Dean? They'll need some breeders. How else are you going to get laid? (*more serious*) Maybe your sister and mom are up there. You ready to act on that Freudian impulse? For the survival of the species?

Theresa: Stop it, Terry. Or I'll leave you right here, right now.

Dean: You should leave him.

Paul: Come on, Terry. Why aren't you going?

Terry: To Canada? I'll give you two reasons, Céline Dion and Justin Bieber.

Dean: What if Theresa wants to go?

Terry looks at Theresa.

Theresa: I told you, I can't go back to the cellar.

Terry looks from Theresa to the bloody coffee cup on the counter.

Terry: It's fuckin' futile.

Theresa: (*takes his hand*) Maybe not. It's proactive.

Terry: I think the word is *radioactive*.

Paul: Not everywhere.

Theresa: Not everyone.

Karl: Not everything.

Dean: Not the café.

Randy: Not the coffee.

Theresa: Not us.

Terry: Not yet. *(to Theresa)* You weren't here for the human piñata.

Karl: We're never going to get away from being human, Terry.

Terry: Not even in Canada? Isn't mediocrity the first step?

Theresa: We don't need to stop being human, we need to start being humane.

Terry: Is that the woman's view?

Theresa: That's *this* woman's view.

Terry: Soon you may be the only woman left.

Theresa: I don't think so. But if I am, I guess I've got a job to do.

She raises her eyebrows, seductively.

Dean: Do you think you can still procreate?

Everyone scowls at Dean.

Just asking.

Theresa: We've got too much love to hole up in some cellar, Terry. And it wouldn't protect us. It would just spoil like everything else.

Terry: Who said anything about love?

Theresa: I did.

She kisses Terry again, this time deeply.

Paul: Hubba hubba.

Karl: The *feminine mystique*.

Terry: *(looks at Theresa)* I need to swing by my place to pick up a few things.

Paul: We can do that on the way out.

Randy: *(sets down his coffee cup)* I can drive.

Terry: You're kidding?

Paul: That's great.

Randy: Somebody has to teach the *real* history of baseball.

Terry: Bullshit. I don't care how heavy it is, I'm bringing my Sports Almanac.

Randy: Statistics only back up my case.

Terry: Teddy Ballgame won the Triple Crown twice! *(holds up two fingers)*

Randy: DiMaggio was MVP three times. (*wiggles three fingers*)

Terry: That's a popularity contest! (*gives Randy the middle finger*)

Paul: This is going to be a long trip.

Paul walks to the counter and sets his cup and saucer next to the cup catching Marcus's blood. One by one, the others put their empty cups in a row on the counter.

Dean: Thank you for bussing your tables.

Terry, Paul, Randy and Theresa gather themselves to leave.

Terry: (*to Karl and Dean*) Are you two going to be all right?

They nod.

Paul: If you change your mind, you know where to find us.

Dean: Canada.

Terry: That should be easy enough. Look for me, I'll be the white guy, *shivering.*

Terry zips up his jacket. Paul gives Karl and Dean a hug, then Randy shakes their hands.

Randy: I'll get my cab.

Paul: I'll go with you.

At the door, Paul stares at the blood-written "Imagine."

110

(to Dean) There's a squeegee next to the mop bucket, if you decide to start cleaning up the outside.

Paul waves goodbye – he exits with Randy.

Terry: *(to Karl)* Don't get caught hot-wiring cars with Dean.

Karl: Don't lose your sunny disposition.

Terry: No promises.

Theresa steps forward, giving Dean a quick kiss on the cheek.

Theresa: Good Luck.

Theresa gives Karl a kiss.

Terry: *(shakes Dean's hand)* You know all that shit I was saying before, I was just joking.

Dean: Really?

Terry: No. But what the fuck? We probably won't ever see each other again.

Outside, a car horn honks.

Karl: You two take care of each other.

Theresa: We will.

Terry: We'll try. You two, don't start mounting any human heads on these walls.

They exit.

Dean walks around the counter, putting on an apron.

Dean: Cup of coffee?

Karl nods.

What do you drink, Karl? Americano? *(starts making coffee)* This will be the first espresso drink I've ever made.

Karl sees a drop of blood drip from the ceiling.

Karl: *(sarcastic)* I can't wait.

The payphone rings.

Dean: Maybe someone's trying to call in an order.

Karl quickly goes to the payphone.

Karl: Hello?

There is a pause – Karl's expression changes.

Oh my God!... How did you? I can't... I can't hear... the signal... the signal... your... Where are you? Are you all right? Is your mother... she... Oh my God!... How... That's why I gave you this number... I said... Oh my... Oh... My sweet sweet little girl... You're so smart... I... I... you're cutting out... you're ... I can't... I... I... I'm right here... I'll be... yes... yes... I'm... Don't cry, dear... I'll be... Yes... Don't cry, my love... It will be... Everything will... You'll... Yes... yes... Get there... Do that... Do that, Shel... I'll be... Shelly... Yes you can... yes... yes... no... no... You have to be strong... You have to be strong... Good people are going there... I know... because I know... Because I'm your father... And I'll... I'll wait for... Until you get there, I'll wait right here at the café for a call... I'll be... I said... I'll... Shel... Shelly, dear... I can't... you're... I said... Listen, Shelly... Can you hear me? Listen to me... Daddy loves you, dear... Shel... Can you hear me?... No matter what happens... you have to... Shel... Shel... please... please... No... No, no, no... Don't... Don't do that, Shel... Don't... Daddy loves... That's not... I can't... you're... listen... listen to me Shel... Listen... I love you, Shelly... I... I... I... Shel?

Karl looks at the receiver in his hand. Then stares out the window at the eerie glow.

Dean: Who was it?

Karl slowly puts the receiver back in its cradle.

Karl: My daughter.

Dean sets Karl's coffee on the counter.

Dean: How did she call the payphone?

As if in a trance, Karl walks to the counter.

Karl: I gave her the number, but...

Dean: But how with all the...

Karl: I don't know, Dean. It was a bad connection. (*to himself*) Shelly's resourceful.

Dean pushes forward the coffee cup toward Karl.

Dean: That's great. Is she in Canada?

113

Karl: No. She's coming here.

Dean: She's coming here?

Karl nods, and takes a sip of his coffee.

Marcus was right. People will always come to the café.

Karl nods again, noncommittally.

How's the Americano?

Karl: It's fine, Dean. Thanks.

Dean: That's two-fifty.

Karl looks at Dean in disbelief.

You can pay when you're finished. I trust you.

Dean smiles, then bends over – disappearing beneath the counter. He appears, holding a squeegee and a bar towel.

Business is going to be thriving soon. And we want everything real clean if your daughter's coming.

Karl watches Dean step around the counter, stopping at a few drops of blood splattered on the floor.

Karl sees a drop of blood fall from the ceiling.

Karl: Give me that towel.

"Business is going to be thriving soon."

Dean hands him the bar towel. Karl wipes up the mess, then looks up at the ceiling. He drains the rest of his coffee in a swallow and sets down the cup – a drip falls into it.

Karl hands Dean the towel, then reseats himself.

Karl: Shelly might try to call again. I'm going to wait.

Dean heads to the front door with the towel and squeegee.

Dean: You can't give up hope

Karl looks at the coffee cup on the floor, catching blood.

People are going to come to the café. *(opens the door)* "With electricity comes responsibility."

Dean steps into the glow outside. He begins to clean the blood-written word "Imagine" off the window, humming the tune to "Imagine" while he works.

Karl watches another drop of blood fall from the ceiling into the cup.

Karl: *(to himself)* My day has started.

CURTAIN.

I would like to thank the following:

My uncle *Bruce Anderson* and *The Anderson Valley Advertiser* for publishing an earlier version of this play in six parts, and including my voice in its pages for over thirty years.

Sandow Birk for his friendship and fearless talent, incredible illustrations, and unflagging willingness to collaborate on this and other projects with me.

Jay Walsh for his friendship, enthusiasm and appreciation for the sublime in all its forms and fonts, and hours of creative design.

Jon Moscone for being an Up Cal "brother in arms" and his ability to give broad notes while also attacking the minutia, not to mention his infectious energy and unending support.

Jim "Little Jimmy Muppet" Isaac for all his help in life, even after his last breath.

The Magic Theater for staging a reading early on in Teddy's maturation.

Domenic Stansberry for creating *Molotov Editions*, shining light in the shadows and margins of low life and high art, and saying "Yes!" to my dark sense of humor.

Caffe Trieste for hiring me when I needed it most, supplying the coffee and the setting.

Also for their help, advice, and support during the writing of *The Death of Teddy Ballgame*, without which this work may have never been completed; *Zack Anderson, David Yearsley, Peter Plate, Thomas Sanchez, Daniel Handler, Les Claypool, Eric Harland, Joshua Redman, Jim Goldberg, Peter Kaufman, Charlie* and *Henrietta Musselwhite, Amy Tan, Shiloh Fernandez, Jay Leahy, Ion Vlad, Tony Barbieri, Tom Barbash, Avishai Cohen, Henri Behar, Scott Bourne, Antonio Lucio, Larry Blum, Jimmy Glover, SFJAZZ, The SFJAZZ Collective, Ben Jealous, Geoffrey Kirkland, Jason Leggiere, Joshua Jennings, Leonardo, Shawn Phillips, Joe Lucas* and *Alex Peer.*

ROBERT MAILER ANDERSON was born in San Francisco and is a 7th generation native "Californio." He is the author of the best-selling novel "Boonville," co-writer/producer of the film "PIG HUNT," and a contributor to *The Anderson Valley Advertiser* since the age of fifteen. His writing has appeared in *San Francisco Noir*, *Zyzzyva*, *Christopher Street*, *Encore*, *San Francisco Magazine*, *The San Francisco Chronicle*, *The Argonaut*, and Ishmael Reed's *Konch*, among other publications. Aside from a strange rash of other seemingly dissimilar occupations, endeavors and accolades, Anderson was a barista at North Beach's historic Caffe Trieste, an SFJAZZ board trustee, a member of President Obama's 2012 National Finance Committee, the 2013 Selkirk Colonial Society Standard Bearer, and a recipient of the 2016 San Francisco Arts Medallion.

Los Angeles artist **SANDOW BIRK** is a well-traveled graduate of the Otis/Parson's Art Institute. Frequently developed as expansive, multi-media projects, his works have dealt with contemporary life in its entirety. With an emphasis on social issues, frequent themes of his past work have included inner city violence, graffiti, political issues, travel, war, and prisons, as well as surfing and skateboarding. He was a recipient of an NEA International Travel Grant in 1995, a Guggenheim Fellowship in 1996, and a Fulbright Fellowship in 1997. In 1999 he was awarded a Getty Fellowship for painting, followed by a City of Los Angeles (COLA) Fellowship in 2001. In 2007 he was an artist in residence at the Smithsonian Institute in Washington, DC, and at the Cité Internationale des Arts in Paris in 2008. His most recent project involves a consideration of the Qur'an as relevant to contemporary life in America.

CPSIA information can be obtained
at www.ICGtesting.com
Printed in the USA
FSOW02n0443111016
25876FS

9 780996 765923